S0-ARS-841

WITHDRAWN

UP
AND
DOWN

AMY CULLIFORD

A Crabtree Roots Book

CRABTREE
Publishing Company
www.crabtreebooks.com

School-to-Home Support for Caregivers and Teachers

This book helps children grow by letting them practice reading. Here are a few guiding questions to help the reader with building his or her comprehension skills. Possible answers appear here in red.

Before Reading:

• What do I think this book is about?
  - *I think this book is about directions.*
  - *I think this book is about what up and down mean.*

• What do I want to learn about this topic?
  - *I want to learn what it looks like when something is up or down.*
  - *I want to learn which objects can go up, and which objects can go down.*

During Reading:

• I wonder why...
  - *I wonder why rain does not go up.*
  - *I wonder why people and animals jump up.*

• What have I learned so far?
  - *I have learned that planes can go up and down.*
  - *I have learned what up and down directions look like.*

After Reading:

• What details did I learn about this topic?
  - *I have learned the Sun comes up and goes down every day.*
  - *I have learned that rain comes down. It does not go up.*

• Read the book again and look for the vocabulary words.
  - *I see the word **cat** on page 3 and the word **Sun** on page 7. The other vocabulary words are found on page 14.*

The **cat** jumps up.

The **dog** sits down.

The **Sun** comes up.

The **rain** comes down.

The **plane** is up.

The plane is down.

Word List

Sight Words

comes	jumps	up
down	sit	
is	the	

Words to Know

cat

dog

plane

rain

Sun

24 Words

The **cat** jumps up.

The **dog** sits down.

The **Sun** comes up.

The **rain** comes down.

The **plane** is up.

The plane is down.

Written by: Amy Culliford
Designed by: Rhea Wallace
Series Development: James Earley
Proofreader: Janine Deschenes
Educational Consultant: Marie Lemke M.Ed.

Photographs:
Shutterstock: Tony Campbell: cover, p. 1; Rita_
    Komarjova: p. 3, 14; NotarYES: p. 5, 14; Symonenko
    Viktoriia: p. 6, 14; ND700: p. 9, 14; RussHeini: p. 11, 14;
    Piotr Mitelski: p. 13

Library and Archives Canada Cataloguing in Publication

CIP available at Library and Archives Canada

Library of Congress Cataloging-in-Publication Data

CIP available at Library of Congress

Crabtree Publishing Company

www.crabtreebooks.com   1-800-387-7650

Copyright © 2022 **CRABTREE PUBLISHING COMPANY**   Printed in the U.S.A./CG20210915/012022

All rights reserved. No part of this publication may be reproduced, stored in a retrieval system or be transmitted in any form or by any means, electronic, mechanical, photocopying, recording, or otherwise, without the prior written permission of Crabtree Publishing Company. In Canada: We acknowledge the financial support of the Government of Canada through the Canada Book Fund for our publishing activities.

Published in the United States
Crabtree Publishing
347 Fifth Avenue, Suite 1402-145
New York, NY, 10016

Published in Canada
Crabtree Publishing
616 Welland Ave.
St. Catharines, Ontario L2M 5V6